APRICOTS TOMORROW

Primrose Arnander Ashkhain Skipwith

with illustrations by
Kathryn Lamb

STACEY INTERNATIONAL
LONDON

By the same authors
The Son of a Duck is a Floater

Published by Stacey International
128 Kensington Church Street
London W8 4BH
Telex 298768 Stacey G
Fax 071-792 9288

ISBN 0 905743 57 1

Set in Plantin by SX Composing Limited, Essex, England.
Set by Aurora Press Ltd., London

British Library Cataloguing in Publication Data
Arnander, Primrose
Apricots Tomorrow
I. Title II. Skipwith, Ashkhain
398′.9′.927

Library of Congress Cataloging-in-Publication Data

Apricots tomorrow/(compiled by) Primrose Arnander, Ashkhain Skipwith: with illustrations by Kathryn Lamb.
"A companion volume to: The Son of a duck is a floater."
English and Arabic
1. Proverbs, Arabic. 2. Proverbs, English. I. Arnander, Primrose. II. Skipwith, Ashkhain.
PN6519.A7H67 1989 89-4553
398.9′927--dc20 CIP

Note on transliteration

The form of transliteration used is one that has been developed over recent years, somewhat simplified in the hope it will help those with little or no Arabic to articulate the proverbs in their original language. Most of the transliterations are self-evident, but a few comments may be useful.

ẓ ṭ ḍ ṣ ḥ	*are hard letters, heavily pronounced*
dh th	*equivalent to th (as in there and think, respectively)*
ā ū ī	*are long (as in baa, moon, seen)*
kh	*equivalent to ch, as in loch*
gh	*rolled, as in the French letter r*
g	represents the Arabic qaaf (hard q)
‘ ’	*before and after letters, represents the Arabic letters ayn (‘) and hamza (’), which have no English equivalent. The exact sound cannot be explained easily in writing, the nearest equivalent being a glottal stop or hesitation.*

Authors' Preface

This, our second collection of Arab proverbs and sayings, is the result of the encouragement and contributions that we received following the publication of our first collection entitled *The Son of a Duck is a Floater*. As with the first book, the proverbs and sayings originate from various parts of the Arab world and have been assembled and presented with an eye to their current colloquial use rather than as a contribution to scholarship.

We have adopted the style of the earlier collection. The Arabic is followed by a transliteration, to make it readable for those unfamiliar with Arabic script. This is followed by a literal English translation and finally, the English equivalent or an acceptable comparison; occasionally, a short explanation is provided where we feel that the sense might not be readily understood.

Kathryn Lamb has once again produced the illustrations which constitute such an important part of the book. Although now settled in the English countryside, she has lost none of her affinity with the Arab world and her cartoons bring pleasure to East and West alike.

Finally, we acknowledge our debt to those readers who sent us their own favourite proverbs as well as to the many friends who helped us with contributions and possible equivalents – they are too many to name individually, but they have our deepest thanks. We are especially grateful to that well known scholar and diplomat, Sir James Craig, who, in addition to providing invaluable help and advice has written the introduction to this volume.

Primrose Arnander   Ashkhain Skipwith

Introduction

The previous collection of Arabic proverbs produced by Primrose Arnander and Ashkhain Skipwith had an obscure title: *The Son of a Duck is a Floater*. The title of the present volume is equally obscure, intriguingly obscure. What on earth, the bookshop browser is meant to ask, can 'Apricots Tomorrow' mean?

Perhaps there is this inherent mystery in proverbs: that though they are supposed to convey a moral or a message, the message is often a puzzle inside a riddle inside an enigma. I remember being perplexed as a boy by my mother's admonition 'You can't have your cake and eat it'. What was the point, I wondered, of having a cake if you couldn't eat it? Then again, are we advised (a) to feed a cold and (b) starve a fever? Or are we being warned that if we feed a cold, the next thing we shall have to treat, as a consequence, will be a fever? And if he who hesitates is lost, why must we look before we leap?

Many of the examples gathered here leave me similarly unsure about what I am being told. I have peddled them round the Middle East and have had different explanations from different friends. Some of these proverbs may puzzle you too, some may strike you as wise and witty. All of them should set you thinking and talking, not only about the advice and sagacity they contain, but also about the differences and the similarities between Arab society and our own. The editors have assembled a rich assortment of mystery and stimulus. If you also find obscurity and inconsistency, that is only the reverse side of the coin. As the old English proverb says, a fly in the ointment is worth two in the bush.

Sir James Craig
London

لو دعاء الكلب يستجاب كان بتشتي الدنيا عظام

Law du ʿā' al-kalb yustajāb, kān bitishtī al-dunyā ʿiẓām

If the dog's prayers were answered, the skies would rain bones

If wishes were horses, beggars would ride

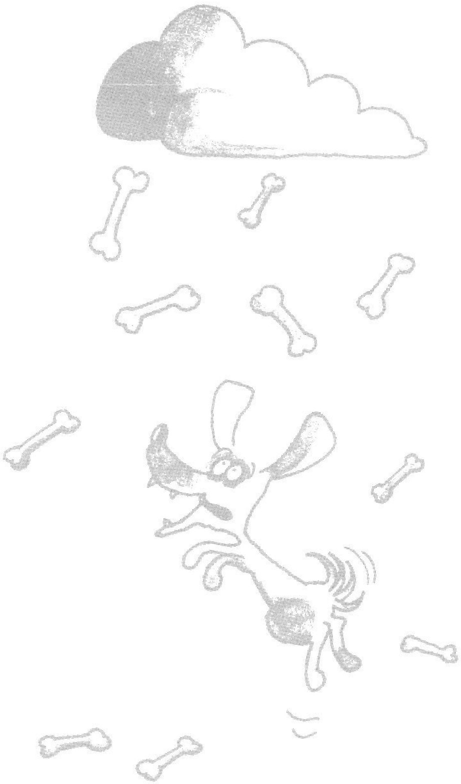

من سدد ديونه نامت عيونه

Man saddad duyūnu nāmat ʻuyūnu

He who has paid his debts can close his eyes

Out of debt, out of danger

إجلس أعوج واحكي دغري

Ijlis aʻwaj wa ihkī dughrī

Sit crooked and speak straight

من حفر حفرة لأخيه وقع فيها

Man ḥafara ḥufratan li-akhīhi waqa'a fīhā

He who digs a hole for his brother will fall into it

Hoist with his own petard

خيرها في غيرها

Khayrhā fī ghayrhā

A *better one in another one*

Better luck next time

مثل أم العروسة

Mithil umm al-ʿarūsa

Like *the bride's mother*

As busy as a hen with one chicken

الأسد في بلاد الغربة جبان

Al-asadu fī bilādi 'l-ghurbati jabān

The lion is a coward in strange lands

إللي مكتوب على الجبين لازم تشوفه العين

Illī maktūb ʻaljabīn lāzim tishūfu al ʻayn

What is written on the forehead, the eye must see

What must be, must be

إللي ياكل على ضرسه ينفع نفسه

Illī yākul ʻala ḍirsu yinfaʻ nafsu

He who chews with his own teeth benefits himself

God helps those who help themselves

كل ديك على مذبلته صيّاح

Kull dīk ʻala mazbalatu ṣayyāḥ

Every cock is a town crier on his own dung heap

Every cock will crow upon his own dunghill

إللي بيجي هيك بروح هيك

Illī bījī hayk birūḥ hayk

What comes this way, goes this way

Easy come, easy go

حج وبياع مسابح

Ḥājj wa bayyā masābiḥ

Both a pilgrim and a seller of prayer beads

To run with the hare and hunt with the hounds

إذا مرض الغزال فلا ترسل الأسد لتشخيص الداء

Idhā mariḍa ghazālun falā tursil al-asada litashkhīṣi 'l-dā'

If a gazelle falls ill do not send the lion to diagnose the complaint

It is a foolish sheep that makes the wolf his confessor

إللي ما بيحضر عنزه ما بتجيب توم

Illī mā yiḥḍar ʿanzu mā bitjīb taw'am

He who does not attend his goats during delivery will not be given twins

Keep your shop and your shop will keep you

كل بيت وفيه بالوعة

Kull bayt wa fīhi bālūʿa

Every house has its sewers

There is a black sheep in every flock

الكلاب تنبح والقافلة تسير

Al-kilāb tanbaḥ wa 'l-qāfila tasīr

The dogs bark, but the caravan moves on

عابوا الورد، قالوا خده أحمر

ʻĀbū ʼl-ward, qālū khaddu aḥmar

They criticised the rose, they said its cheek was red

You find fault with a fat goose

كل مين يقرب النار بقرصه

Kull mīn yiqarrib an-nār biqurṣu

Everyone puts his own loaf as close as he can to the fire

To take care of number one

انفرطت المسبحة

Infaraṭat al-masbaḥa

The prayer beads have come unstrung

The fat is in the fire

ستين سنة سبعين يوم

Sittīn sana sab ʻīn yawm

Sixty years, seventy days

It's six of one, half a dozen of the other

قال إيش أرخص من العسل، الخل ببلاش

Qāl aysh arkhaṣ min al-ʻasal, al-khal bibalāsh

He asked 'What could be cheaper than honey?' – vinegar is free

If you pay peanuts, you get monkeys

كل حلة فيها علة

Kull ḥulla fīhā ʻilla

Every garment has a fault

Nothing is perfect

سمحناله، فات وفوّت حماره

Samaḥnā lahu, fāt wa fawwat ḥimāru

We let him in and he brought his donkey too

Give him an inch and he'll take an ell

كل عقدة ولها حلال

Kull ʿuqda wa lahā ḥallāl

Every knot has someone to undo it

Every problem has a solution

ما بعد الضيق إلا الفرج

Mā baʿd aḍ-ḍīq illā ʾl-faraj

There is nothing after hardship except repose

After a storm comes a calm

إذا ما قطع فيها القدوم، يقطع فيها المنشار

Idhā mā qaṭa‘a fīhā ’l-qaddūm yiqṭa‘ fīhā ’l-munshār

If the hammer does not break it, the saw will cut it

There’s more ways than one to kill a cat

عند العقدة وقف النجار

'Ind al-'uqda waqaf al-najjār

At the knot the carpenter stopped

To throw in the towel at the first count

A boxing metaphor

ما في شي ببلاش ولا العمى والطراش

Mā fī shay bibalāsh wala al-'amā wa 'ṭ-ṭirāsh

Nothing is for free, not even blindness and deafness

There is no such thing as a free lunch

أكل العنب حبة حبة

Akl al-ʿinab ḥabba ḥabba

Grapes are eaten one by one

One step at a time

إذا كنت كذوباً فكن ذكوراً

Idhā kunta kadhūban fa kun dhakūra

If you want to be a liar, better have a good memory

Liars need good memories

المال السايب يعلم السرقة

Al-māl as-sāyib yi'allim as-sirqah

Unattended money teaches theft

Opportunity makes the thief

حامض يا عنب

Idhā ba'ad al-'unqūd qāl ḥāmiḍ yā'inab

Sour grapes!

بكرة في المشمش

Bukra fil mishmish

Tomorrow there will be apricots

Tomorrow never comes

‘Jam tomorrow and jam yesterday, but never jam today.’
(*Alice Through the Looking Glass,* Lewis Carroll)

مزيّن بسط على أقرع استفتح

Muzayyin basaṭ ʿalā aqraʿ istaftaḥ

The barber opened up his shop; his first customer was bald

To start the day off on the wrong foot

ما على الكريم تشترط

Mā ʿala ʾl-karīm tisharriṭ

Do not bind the generous man with conditions

Never look a gift horse in the mouth

راحت تبغي قرون، جاءت بلا أذون

Rāḥat tabghī qurūn, jāʿat bilā udhūn

She went looking for horns and returned home without ears

Many go out for wool and come home shorn

ما تجيبه الريح تاخده الزوابع

Mā tijību ar-rīḥ tākhdu az-zawābi'

What the wind brings the storm takes away

Fortune is fickle

ألف سبة ما تشق ثوب

Alf sabba mā tashuq thawb

A thousand curses do not tear a robe

Sticks and stones may break my bones,
But words will never hurt me

العنزة تعلم أمها الرضاعة

Al-'anza ti'allim ummahā 'r-riḍā'a

The kid teaches its mother to suckle

Necessity is the mother of invention

ما في شجرة ما هزّها الهوا

Mā fī shajara mā hazzahā 'l-hawā

There is not a tree that has not been swayed by the breeze

Every man has his price

ابعد عن الشر وغني له

Ib'id 'an ash-sharr wa ghannī lu

Keep away from trouble and sing to it

Never trouble trouble till trouble troubles you

يا سارق الديك فوق راسك الريش

Yā sāriq ad-dīk fawq rāsak ar-rīsh

You stole the cockerel, the feather is on your head

cf. *To be caught red-handed*

تيتي تيتي مثل ما رحتي مثل ما جيتي

Tītī tītī mithil mā ruhṭī mithil mā jītī

As you went, so you came back

So what else is new!

اصرف ما في الجيب يأتي ما في الغيب

Iṣrif mā fil jayb ya'ṭīk mā fil ghayb

Spend what is in your pocket; you will get more from the unknown

Spend and God will send

بيضة اليوم أحسن من ديك بكره

Bayḍat al-yawm aḥsan min dīk bukra

Today's egg is better than tomorrow's cockerel

Better an egg today than a hen tomorrow

حرّسوا القط على اللبن

Ḥarrasū 'l-qiṭṭ 'alā al-laban

They left the cat to guard the milk

They set the wolf to guard the sheep
'Alas poor Proteus! Thou hast entertained
A fox to be the shepherd of thy lamb.' (*Two Gentlemen of Verona*, William Shakespeare)

بنت البيت عورة

Bint al-bayt ʻawra

The daughter of the house is one-eyed

cf. *The grass is greener on the other side*
Traditionally men are expected to limit their choice of bride from among their cousins

خلي البطيخ يكسر بعضه

Khallī 'l-baṭṭīkh yikassir baʻḍu

Let the water melons break each other

Let them stew in their own juice

المكان ضيّق والحمار رفّاص

Al-makān ḍayyiq wa 'l-ḥimār raffāṣ

The room is small and the donkey is a kicker

This place is too small for both of us

ضرْب الحبيب زبيب

Ḍarb al-ḥabīb zabīb

Beatings by a loved one are as sweet as raisins

cf. *The falling out of faithful friends is the renewing of love*
(Richard Edwardes 1523-1566)

سحب السجاد من تحت رجله

Saḥab as-sijjād min taḥt rijlu

He pulled the carpet from under his feet

A proverb shared by both languages

أخذ القرد لماله، راح المال وبقي القرد على حاله

Akhad al-qird limālu, rāḥ al-māl wa baqā 'l-qird 'alā ḥālu

He married the monkey for its money, the money went and the monkey stayed a monkey

As you make your bed, so you must lie on it

عدم الجواب جواب

ʿAdam al-jawāb jawāb

No *answer is an answer*

Silence speaks volumes

جمرة في القلب ولا دمعة في العين

Jamra fil qalb walā damʿa fil ʿayn

A fire in the heart but no tear in the eye

To keep a stiff upper lip

يا داخل بين البصلة وقشرتها ما نابك إلا صنتها

Yā dākhil bayn al-baṣala wa qishrit-hā, mā nābak illā ṣannit-hā

Whoever gets between the onion and its skin will only be rewarded by its stink

Never get between a man and his wife

الكلام له طعم مثل الطعام

Al-kalām lahu ṭa'm mithl aṭ-ṭa'ām

Talk has a taste like food

Watch your tongue!

أهل مكة أدرى بشعابها

Ahl Makka adrā bishi 'ābihā

The people of Makkah know their own streets best

To know somewhere like the back of your hand.

أعطي الخبز للخباز ولو أكل نصفه

A'ṭī al khubz lil khabbāz wa akal niṣfu

Give the bread to the baker even if he eats half of it

The labourer is worthy of his hire

حجر في دكان الزّجاج

Ḥajar fī dukkān az-zajjāj

A stone in the shop of a glass merchant

A bull in a china shop

ذنبك على جنبك

Dhanbak ʻalā janbak

Your guilt stands at your side

A guilty conscience needs no accuser

الجاهل عدو نفسه

Al-jāhil ʻadū nafsu

The ignorant person is his own enemy

'A little learning is a dangerous thing.' (*Essay on Criticism*, Alexander Pope, 1711)

الثوب المستعار لا يدفّي

Ath-thawb al musta'ār lā yudaffī

The borrowed robe doesn't keep out the cold

Borrowed garments never fit well

إذا طامت البقرة كثرت سكاكينها

Idhā ṭāmat al baqara kathirat sakākīnhā

If the cow falls, the knives multiply

To kick someone when they are down

الفاضي يعمل قاضي

Al-fāḍī yiʿmal qāḍī

The idle man makes himself a judge

An armchair critic

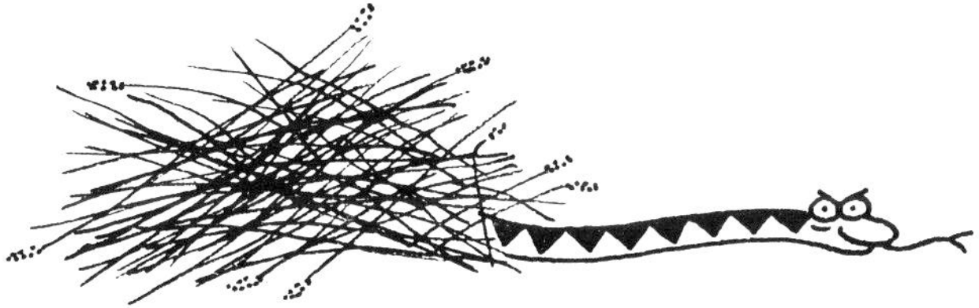

مثل الحية تحت التبن

Mithl al-ḥayya taḥt at-tibn

Like a snake under the hay

Like a snake in the grass

على المؤذن أن يؤذن

'Ala 'l-mu'adhdhin an yu'adhdhin

It is the business of the muezzin to call to prayers

Let the cobbler stick to his last

الحيطان لها أودان

Al-ḥīṭān lahā awdān

Walls have ears

A proverb shared by both languages

يا مسترخص اللحم عند المرق تندم

Yā mistarkhiṣ al laḥm ʻīnd al-maraq tindam

If you buy cheap meat you will be sorry when you come to the gravy

Beware of false economy

بعد العود ما في قعود

Ba'd al-'ūd mā fī qu'ūd

After the incense is passed there is no sitting on

Don't overstay your welcome
When a visit has lasted long enough the host passes round the incense signifying that it's time for his guests to leave

الأعور في بلاد العميان طرفة

Al-aʻwar fī bilād al-ʻumyān ṭurfa

The one-eyed person is a beauty in the country of the blind

In the country of the blind, the one-eyed man is king

بير تشرب منه لا ترمي فيه حجر

Bīr tishrab minhu lā tarmī fīhi ḥajar

Into the well from which you drink, do not throw a stone

It's a foolish bird that fouls its own nest

حبة تثقل الميزان

Ḥabba tithaqqil al-mīzān

A single grain tips the scales

It is the last straw that breaks the camel's back

يمينك ما يدري عن يسارك

Yamīnak mā yadrī ʻan yasārak

Your right hand doesn't know what your left hand is doing

A proverb shared by both languages

لسان التجربة أصدق

Lisān at-tajriba aṣdaq

The tongue of experience is more truthful

Experience is the best teacher

غابت السباع ولعبت الضباع

Ghābat as-sibāʿ wa laʿibat al ḍibaʿ

When the lions were absent, the hyenas played

When the cat's away, the mice will play

القصاب لا تهوله كثرة الغنم

Al qaṣṣāb lā tuhawwilu kathrat al-ghanam

The butcher is not alarmed by the multitude of sheep

The more the merrier

الميه تكذب الغطاس

Al-mayya tikadhdhib al-ghaṭṭāṣ

The water shows up the diver

cf. *The proof of the pudding is in the eating*

ادخلوا البيوت من أبوابها

Udkhulū 'l-buyūt min abwābihā

Enter houses by their front doors

Don't go behind people's backs

يوم عسل ويوم بصل

Yawm ʻasal wa yawm baṣal

One day honey, one day onions

One must take the rough with the smooth

أطول من شهر الصّوم

Aṭwal min shahr aṣ-ṣawm

Longer than the fasting month

Longer than a month of Sundays

كلمة يا ريت لا تعمر بيت

Kilmit yā rayt lā ṭi ʻammir bayt

The words 'I wish' build no houses

If ifs and ans were pots and pans, there'd be no trade for tinkers

ضرب عصفورين بحجر

Ḍarab ʻuṣfūrayn biḥajar

He struck two birds with one stone

To kill two birds with one stone

من طلب العلى سهر الليالي

Man ṭalaba 'l-'ulā sahira 'l-layālī

He who seeks higher things stays awake at nights

'Uneasy lies the head that wears a crown.' (*King Henry IV Part 2*, William Shakespeare)

الغربال الجديد له شدّة

Al-ghurbāl al-jadīd lahu shadda

The new sieve is taut

A new broom sweeps clean

كلب ينبح لا يعض

Kalb yanbaḥ lā ya ʻaḍḍ

A dog that barks does not bite

His bark is worse than his bite

صاحب الحق له مقام وله مقال

Ṣāḥib al-ḥaq lahu maqām wa lahu maqāl

The man who is in the right has both stature and the last word

The best argument is to be right

الدراهم مراهم

Ad-darāhim marāhim

Money is a salve

Ready money is a ready medicine

حلم القطط كله فيران

Ḥilm al-quṭaṭ kullu fīrān

The dream of cats is all mice

To have a one track mind

راح الخيط والعصفور

Rāḥ al-khayṭ wal 'uṣfūr

Both the line and the bird have gone

It's gone – hook, line and sinker

الصبر مر وثمرته حلوة

Aṣ-ṣabr murr wa thamaratu ḥilwa

Patience is bitter but its fruit is sweet

cf. *Patience is a remedy for every sorrow*

بصلة الحبيب وليمة

Baṣalat al-ḥabīb walīma

A *loved one's onion is a feast*

Better dry bread with your darling than butter with your boss

أكل الجمل بما حمل

Akal al-jamal bi mā ḥamal

He ate the camel and all it carried

To eat someone out of house and home

الصديق لوقت الضيق

Aṣ-ṣadīq liwaqt aḍ-ḍīq

A true friend is for the time of trouble

A friend in need is a friend indeed

الغريق يتعلق بقشة

Al-gharīq yit'allaq bi-qashsha

A drowning man clutches at a straw

A proverb shared by both languages

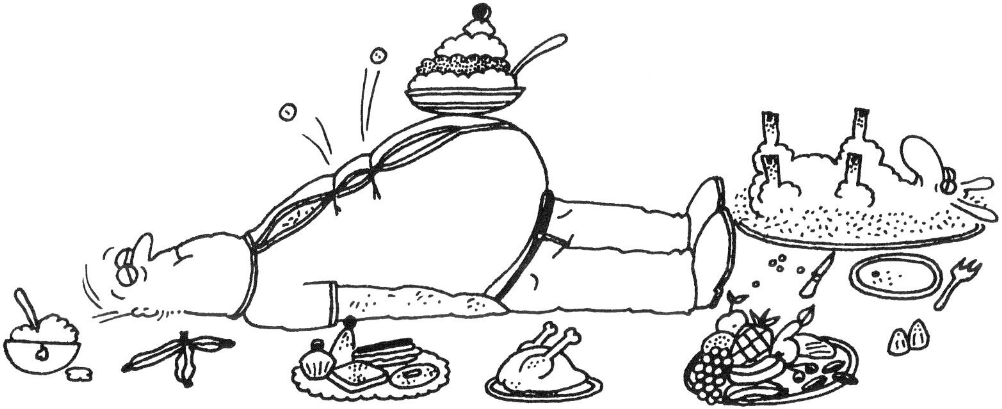

طمعه قتله

Ṭamaʻu qatalu

His *greed killed him*

Gluttony kills more than the sword

يزيد من الطين بلة

Yazīd min aṭ-ṭīn balla

Add wetness to the mud

Add fuel to the fire

الصراحة راحة

Aṣ-ṣarāḥa rāḥa

Frankness is peace of mind

cf. *Speak the truth and shame the devil*

اللي أمه في الدار قرصه حار

Illī ummu fi ad dār qurṣu ḥār

When a man's mother is at home, his loaf of bread is warm

A mother's care is best of all

رحلة الألف ميل تبدأ بخطوة

Riḥlat al-alf mīl tabda' bikhaṭwa

A journey of a thousand miles starts with one step

cf. *From small beginnings come great things*

الشاطرة تغزل برجل حمار

Ash shāṭra tighzil birijl ḥimār

The clever woman could spin with a donkey's foot

To be equal to anything

ربنا يبعث اللوز للي ما له أسنان

Rabbanā yab ʻath al-lawz li ʼllī mā lahu asnān

The Lord sends almonds to those without teeth

Good things come when we are too old to enjoy them

العين بصيرة واليد قصيرة

Al-'ayn baṣīra wa 'l-yadd qaṣīra

The eye sees but the hand does not reach

A moneyless man goes fast through the market

كل فولة مسوسة لها كيّال أعور

Kull fūla musawwisa lahā kayyāl a'war

Every decayed bean has a one-eyed man to weigh it

cf. *Everyone finds his own level*

طب الجرة على تمها تطلع البنت لأمها

Ṭub al-jarra ʿala tumhā tiṭlaʿ al-bint li-ummhā

Turn the earthen pot upside down, the girl will still be like her mother

Like mother, like daughter

مقدمــة

للمجموعة الأولى من الأمثال العربية التي اعدتها المسز ارناندر مع الليدي سكيبويث عنوان غريب هو (ابن البط عوام)، ولكن عنوان المجموعة الثانية هذه لا يقل غرابة فهو بالاضافة الى غرابته غامض وله رنين عجيب. ولا استغرب اذا وقف القارىء الانجليزي على هذا العنوان متأملا ومتسائلا، ترى ما هو المقصود من هذا القول!.

قد يجب المرء في الأمثال أبعادا شاسعة ومعاني عميقة، كما انه من المفروض ان تنقل لنا حكمة رشيدة أو تسدى نصيحة مفيدة. الا ان تلك الحكمة أو النصيحة غالبا ما تكون ملفوفة في غلاف من الكلمات المبهمة التي تشبه التعويذة أو الاحجية. وأذكر عندما كنت طفلا كيف كنت اتوقف مستغربا من العبارة التي كانت تقولها لي والدتي: (لا يمكنك يا بني ان تحافظ على كعكتك وتأكلها في آن واحد) وهو مثل انجليزي معروف وكنت أكرر العبارة في ذهني مرات عديدة فلا افهمها وأقول لنفسي (ما الفائدة من كعكة لا استطيع ان آكلها). وهنا مثال آخر في هذا الشأن قد يوضح ما أعنيه هنا وهو قول المثل الانجليزي «اطعم الزكام وأجع الحمى» فكنت أظن في ذلك الحين ان المعنى المقصود هو اننا اذا اطعمنا الزكام وجب علينا اجاعة الحمى. واذكر ايضا مثلا اخر يقول (المتردد لا بد أن يفشل) ومع ذلك فثمة مثل آخر يعطينا معنى معاكسا وهو «أنظر جيدا قبل ان تقفز». فايهما الصحيح وبأيهما نقتدي.

معظم هذه الأمثال الواردة هنا تجعلني مترددا في قبول المعاني العميقة المقصودة من وراء الأمثال. وقد سألت الكثيرين في شتى أنحاء العالم العربي عن معانيها ومراميها فحصلت على تفاسير كثيرة ومتنوعة. وقد يرى المرء غرابة في بعض الأمثال كما قد يعجب ببعضها الآخر وقد يجد فيها حكمة وذكاء خارقين. انما كل الأمثال كفيلة بأن تحقق امرا واحدا ان لم تحقق سواه وهو ان تجعلك تفكر وتتأمل ليس فقط بالنسبة للنصيحة أو التوجيه أو الارشاد الذي ترمي اليه ولكن ايضا بالنسبة للتشابه والفوارق بين مفاهيم المجتمع العربي والمجتمع البريطاني. وقد تم هنا تشكيل مجموعة طيبة من الأمثال التي ستثير الدهشة والاستغراب وتحفز المرء على التفكير. اما اذا وجد القارىء ابهاما او تضاربا بين مثل واخر فعليه ان يتقبل هذا بصدر رحب لأن هذا من طبيعة الحال. وكما قال المثل الانجليزي القديم (الذبابة في الزيت تساوي اثنتين على الشجرة).

السير جيمس كريج

لنـدن

ولا يمكننا ان نذكر جميع اسمائهم لأنهم كثيرون انما لا يمنعنا هذا من أن نقدم لهم أعمق آيات الشكر والتقدير والامتنان.

ولا بد لنا أيضا ان نشكر بصورة خاصة السير جيمس كريج الاستاذ المعروف والدبلوماسي الكبير، فقد أسدى لنا مساعدات قيّمة وقدّم لنا نصائح جليلة كما انه تفضل مشكورا بكتابة المقدمة لهذا الكتاب.

بريمروز ارناندر   اشخين سكيبويث

مقدمــة من المؤلفتــين

هذه مجموعتنا الثانية من الأمثال والأقوال السائرة العربية. وهي نتاج التشجيع الكبير والمشاركة التي لقيناها على اثر نشر مجموعتنا الأولى (ابن البط عوام). وقد نهجنا في هذا الكتاب على غرار نهجنا في الكتاب الأول، فجمعنا الأمثال والأقوال من شتى البلاد العربية وقدمناها للقارىء تقديما لطيفا وسهلا باستعمالاتها اليومية الشائعة المعروفة وليس على أساس انها ابحاث ودراسات خاصة.

لقد سلكنا نفس السلوك الذي اتبعناه في المجموعة الأولى، فبدأنا أولا بالعبارة العربية للمثل وجعلنا بعد ذلك لفظها العربي بالأحرف اللاتينية ثم ترجمنا المعنى الى اللغة الانجليزية وأوردنا في كل حالة مثلا انجليزيا شائعا معناه قريب من معنى المثل العربي. واذا رأينا في بعض الحالات ان المعنى قد يغيب فحواه عن القارىء أوردنا تفسيرا قصيرا يزيده جلاء وايضاحا.

وقامت السيدة (كاثرين لام) مرة أخرى برسم الصور التوضيحية لهذا الكتاب. ولا شك ان صورها هذه تشكل جزءا رئيسيا من اخراج الكتاب وجماله الكلي. ومع انها تعيش الآن في الريف الانجليزي الا انها لم تفقد شعورها بالقرب الروحي من العالم العربي وستبقى رسوماتها الفكهة تدخل السرور والبهجة على قلوب الجميع في الشرق والغرب على السواء.

وأخيرا، نود ان نشكر بصورة خاصة جميع القرّاء الذين تكرموا علينا بارسال امثالهم المفضلة، كما نشكر اولئك الاصدقاء الذين ساعدونا بمساهمتهم القيمة لانجاز هذا العمل ولايجاد الامثال الانجليزية القريبة من الأصل العربي.

لنفس المؤلفتين
ابن البط عوام

من منشورات ستايسي الدولية
١٢٨ كنسنجتون تشيرتش ستريت
لندن W8 4BH
تلكس ٢٩٨٧٦٨ ستايسي G
فاكس ٩٢٨٨ ٠٧١-٧٩٢

ISBN ٠ ٩٠٥٧٤٣ ٥٧ ١

صف الحروف الانجليزية: شركة إس اكس كومبوزينج ليمتد،
صف الحروف العربية: أورورا برس ليمتد، لندن

طريقة تبويب الكتاب في المكتبة البريطانية، قسم (Publication Data)
بريموز ارناندر
بكرة في المشمش
(١) العنوان (٢) اشخين سكيبويث
٣٩٨ـ٩ـ٩٢٧

التبويب في مكتبة الكونجرس قسم (Publication Data)

بكرة في المشمش/ (اعداد) بريموز ارناندر و اشخين سكيبويث: مع رسوم بريشة كاثرين لام.
«هذا الكتاب ملحق لكتاب مثيل: ابن البط عوام» انجليزي وعربي
١ـ امثال عربية. ٢ـ امثال انجليزية (أ) بريموز ارناندر (ب) اشخين سكيبويث.
PN6519.A7H67 1989 89-4553
398.9'927-dc20 CIP

بكـــرة في المشـمـش

بريمروز أرناندر

اشخين سكيبويث

الصـور بريشـة
كاثـرين لام

مؤسســة ستايسي الدوليـة
لنــدن